THE AUTOMOBILE

Titles in the Inventions
That Changed Our Lives series

N

INVENTIONS THAT CHANGED OUR LIVES

The
Automobile

By Barbara Ford

Walker and Company
New York

First published in the United States of America in 1987 by
the Walker Publishing Company, Inc.

Published simultaneously in Canada by Thomas Allen & Son
Canada, Limited, Markham, Ontario.

Book design by Ellen Pugatch

Library of Congress Cataloging-in-Publication Data

Ford, Barbara.
    The automobile.

    (Inventions that changed our lives)
    Includes index.
    Summary: Traces the invention and development of
the automobile and how it has changed the world around
us.
    1. Automobiles—Juvenile literature.
[1. Automobiles] I. Title. II. Series.
TL147.F59 1987   629.2'22   87-13370
ISBN 0-8027-6722-2
ISBN 0-8027-6723-0 (lib. bdg.)

Printed in the United States of America

10 9 8 7 6 5 4 3 2 1

Contents

Acknowledgments

MY THANKS TO the following for searching their files for illustrative material: Calspan Corporation, Daimler-Benz, Exxon Corporation, Ford Motor Company, General Motors (particularly the Oldsmobile Division), the German Information Center (New York City), Indianapolis Motor Speedway, Michigan Department of Transportation, National Park Service, Peugeot, Rolls-Royce Motors, Southdale Center, U.S. Department of Transportation, Volkswagen of America.

Karl Benz's first automobile had only three wheels. Its top speed was nine miles an hour. *Daimler-Benz*

1

The Horseless Carriage

ON A SPRING DAY in 1885, Karl Benz, a forty-one-year-old German engineer, sat in a machine that looked like a giant tricycle. It had three bicycle wheels, one in front and two in the back. Two mechanics who worked in Benz's machine shop turned a big horizontal wheel—a flywheel—placed just behind the seat. There was a rumbling sound and the strange looking tricycle began to move slowly across the yard of Benz's machine shop. Bertha Benz, Karl's wife, ran beside the machine, clapping her hands.

Suddenly one of the chains that ran from the gasoline-powered engine to the rear wheels burst. The first automobile ride was over.

Benz climbed down, beaming. "Today the horse is through on the highway," he cried.

Benz was a little too optimistic. It took until about 1910 before the horse really was through on the highway. But the tricycle that chugged across the yard in Mannheim, Germany, in 1885 was the beginning of the end for horse-drawn carriages. Benz's invention is accepted by most people as the first automobile powered by an internal combustion engine, the kind of engine we use today.

Benz made improvements in his machine, and on January 29, 1886, he received a patent for the tricycle. By 1888, he was advertising his "motor car" for sale. There were no buyers. In 1886, everyone who could afford one had a horse-drawn carriage. For long-distance travel, there was always the railroad. No one believed Benz's funny-looking machine was practical.

No one, that is, except the Benz family. Benz had taught Bertha and the couple's two teenage sons, Eugen and Richard, how to operate the tricycle. One morning in 1888, while Karl was sleeping, Bertha, Eugen, and Richard decided to drive the latest version of the tricycle to Bertha's hometown, about sixty miles away. They would show people that the machine was practical!

Eugen Benz, 15, took the tiller, a long rod used for steering. Soon they were in trouble. The vehicle, which had less than one horsepower and only one speed, couldn't climb a steep hill. Bertha steered while the two sons pushed the lightweight vehicle up the steepest hills. Then they ran out of fuel. There were no service stations, of course, but they found a druggist who sold them petroleum used for cleaning.

Before long, the party noticed that the leather-lined brakes weren't working. A shoemaker relined them. Next one of the chains that ran from the engine to the wheels came loose. A blacksmith repaired it. Bertha herself cleaned a clogged fuel line with one of her hairpins.

Finally, as Karl Benz reports in his memoirs, the three reached their destination just as night was falling. The sixty-mile trip had taken all day! When Bertha and the boys described the motor car's troubles to Karl later, he realized it still needed more work. One change was made quickly: a lower speed for hills.

The long-distance trip made by the Benz family was the beginning of a change in Karl Benz's fortunes. The following year, a French bicycle manufacturer placed an order for some Benz motor cars. Later the firm encouraged Benz to bring out a four-wheeled motor car.

Meanwhile, another German engineer, Gottlieb Daimler, was developing a gas-powered motorcycle. He received a patent for it shortly before Benz received his own patent. A few months later, Daimler invented the first four-wheeled automobile. Daimler and Benz lived only 60 miles apart, but they never met.

Benz's tricycle and Daimler's motorcycle were the first gas-powered machines to run on the road. Since most of today's automobiles use gas, too, that

Karl and Bertha Benz in a later model of his automobile. It has four wheels. *Daimler-Benz*

makes the German vehicles the closest ancestors to our modern car. But they weren't the first machines to move down a road under their own power.

In 1770, a Frenchman, Joseph Cugnot, invented a machine that used a steam engine to pull a heavy gun. A steam engine burns fuel to heat water, which it changes into steam. The steam is then used to push or spin the parts of a machine. For over a hundred years—from the mid-eighteenth century to the late nineteenth century—steam power was the major source of power throughout the world.

Cugnot's machine, which is now on display in a

An advertisement for Benz's three-wheeled automobile. *German Information Center*

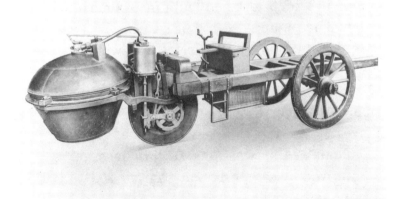

The drawing that appeared on the patent Benz received in 1886. *Daimler-Benz*

5

French museum, was never put to use. By the early 1800s, though, there were a number of efficient steam engines moving carriages along the roads in European countries. In England, one enterprising man even started a bus service using steam-powered carriages.

The railroads, which came into use in the early 1800s, drove these early steam vehicles out of business for a while. Then, just before Karl Benz invented his gasoline-powered motor car, improved steam-powered vehicles made a comeback. About the same time, a new kind of horseless carriage came on the scene: the electric automobile. In 1899, Frenchman Camille Jenatzy drove a bullet-shaped electric auto sixty-five miles per hour in a race.

The first inventor to receive a patent for an internal combustion engine was a Belgian, Etienne Lenoir. By 1862, Lenoir was using his engine in a small carriage. It went only four miles per hour.

Inside Lenoir's engine was a can-shaped container in which a rod called a piston moved up and down. The up-and-down motion was changed into a spinning motion by means of a flywheel, a heavy metal wheel like the one Benz was later to use on his tricycle. Belts and chains carried the spinning motion to the parts of the machine and made them move.

None of this was new. In fact, most of Lenoir's engine was based on steam engines that had been around for many years.

But his engine was different from a steam engine in that the piston was made to move by means

Gottfried Daimler (rear) and his son Adolf ride in the first four-wheeled automobile. Adolf uses the tiller to steer. *Daimler-Benz*

of tiny explosions within the can-shaped container, or cylinder. Another name for explosion is combustion. The gasoline-powered engine is called the "internal combustion" engine because these explosions take place inside the cylinder, which means they are "internal." (The opposite of internal is external.)

In Lenoir's engine, coal, gas, and air were combined and then exploded with an electric spark. Later Lenoir used gasoline, the fuel we use today.

The first internal combustion engine wasn't very efficient. For one thing, it used too much gas. But it gave a German engineer, Nikolas Otto, an idea for a new version. Otto and Gottlieb Daimler, who worked for Otto at that time, introduced their internal combustion engine in 1876. It became the most popular gasoline engine in the world.

The most important change in the new engine

The Panhard & Levassor automobile was the first automobile that looked like an automobile. *Free Library of Philadelphia*

was that the piston went up and down four times for every explosion instead of two, as in the Lenoir engine. As the piston moved, it squeezed the fuel into a smaller space, producing a bigger explosion. All this happened at great speed. Four-cycle engines are still used in most automobiles today.

Before the nineteenth century was over, autos built by a number of inventors were on the road in Europe. Two Frenchman, René Panhard and Emile Levassor, made important contributions to the development of the automobile. In the P & L design, the engine was in the front, under a hood, instead of in the rear, and the power was delivered to the rear wheels. The design had gears to change speed and a clutch to control the gears.

Emile Levassor claimed they had gotten the idea for the Système Panhard, as it was called, from lathes in their woodworking factory. "Brutal," he said, which means crude or rough. But the Système Panhard worked so well we still use it today in our automobiles. Not only that, but it changed the way autos looked. Before, autos looked like carriages without horses.

From this point on, they looked like autos.

2

Bumps and Dust

WHAT WAS IT LIKE riding in one of the early automobiles?

It wasn't much like riding in a modern car. First of all, you had to wear special clothes. Long coats, long gloves, tight-fitting hats, scarves. You had to wear all this because most of the early cars had no tops or windshields. And since most roads at that time were dirt, it was dusty. The driver usually wore a pair of goggles to protect the eyes.

It was cold, too, because early cars had no heaters. Most people didn't even bother to drive in the winter.

When you got into an auto in those days you couldn't just drive away. If it was an internal combustion auto, you had to crank the engine to get it to start. First you adjusted a device that prevented the engine from backfiring. If you didn't do this, the crank would suddenly jerk backward while you were turning it. Some people broke their arms this way.

The Sears, Roebuck catalog for 1902 sold special clothes for riding in automobiles. *Sears, Roebuck, and Co.*

11

The Freerichs family and their Buick in San Diego in 1910.
Charles Freerichs Collection

Then you grabbed the crank, a long rod hanging down from the front of the auto, and turned. And turned and turned and turned. Rumble, rumble! when you heard this noise it meant the flywheel attached to the pistons was spinning. Then the pistons would move up and down, starting the process of internal combustion. Once the engine was running, it would continue by itself.

You're ready to go. Early autos were high, like horse-drawn carriages, so you had to climb up into them. Steering wheels came into use about 1900. The driver sat on the right, not the left. Left-hand steering didn't become popular until about 1908.

It was a bumpy ride! Air-filled pneumatic tires came into use about 1900, but the big balloon tires that cushion the shocks of the road were still in the future. Another thing that made for a rough ride was the fact that early cars had only one or two cylinders. The explosions of the internal combustion engine were far apart, producing a series of jerks.

By our standards, a ride in one of these early autos would be very slow. Speeds averaged about fifteen miles per hour in the first years of the twentieth century.

It was a good thing the early autos didn't go very fast because their brakes were very poor. Brakes were usually operated by hand and connected only to the rear wheels. If you tried to brake on a hill, you might start sliding backward.

There were special problems in those days, too. Most horses pulling carriages on the road were afraid of autos. When an auto driver saw a horse, he had to slow down. The driver of the carriage would usually leap down and grab the horse's head. As you moved slowly by, the horse would often rear up. Sometimes horses ran away.

Many towns and cities passed laws to protect horse-drawn carriages and their occupants. One law required that an automobile driver phone ahead to each town on the route the auto would take. Another required a man with a red flag to walk in front of each auto. Of course, these ridiculous laws made auto drivers angry.

Some auto drivers had their own solutions. One man in Ohio mounted a large wooden head of a horse

Horses were afraid of automobiles. *Oldsmobile Division*

on his auto! But as far as we know, it didn't do much good.

Another special problem was repairs. Early autos often broke down, since auto parts hadn't been perfected. With few repair garages around, an auto owner had to be prepared to handle repairs personally. The worst repair problem was tires. Every automobile ride of any distance was likely to include at least one flat. Not only that, but tires were hard to repair.

When a tire went flat, you had to take the tire off the wheel and remove the inner tube. Drivers carried a little kit with them to repair these tubes.

But a horse came in handy when you got stuck in the mud.
Oldsmobile Division

They heated a patch of rubber and stuck it on the place where the tube had been punctured. Then the tube was pushed back in the tire and pumped up, and the whole apparatus was wrestled back on the rim.

All this took a long time. While you were working, horses and carriages would trot by you. One of the drivers would usually shout: "Get a horse!"

In spite of these problems, most people who used automobiles liked them. They had two big advantages over other forms of transportation: speed and flexibility. Autos were much faster than horses and much more flexible than the train. The fastest a team of horses could average on a good road was about twelve miles per hour. And, of course, the horses couldn't keep up that pace for long. They had to rest.

Trains could go faster than the earliest autos, but they had to run on a track. Even if the town or city you were visiting was near a train station, you still had to use a horse to reach your final destination. Many towns were far from a station, particularly in a big country like the United States. Not only that, but you had to travel on the train's schedule.

With an auto, you could travel when you wanted, where you wanted. And you could go so fast that a trip that used to take a day would be over in a few hours.

At the turn of the century—1900—people were using all three types of autos: steam, electric, and gasoline. The gasoline-powered automobile was no more popular than the steam or electric automobile. Most people, in fact, believed that the steam or electric automobile would be the car of the future.

The gasoline-powered auto? Too noisy, too rattly, too smelly, too slow, people said.

People were wrong.

The gasoline-powered auto improved. Very soon autos powered by gasoline went faster than the steam or electric autos. They handled hills and poor roads better, too. If you ran out of gasoline, you could buy more at the general store found in almost every town. General stores sold gasoline for heating fuel

You stepped up into this 1902 Oldsmobile, which had a cloth top for use when it rained. It was steered with a tiller. *Oldsmobile Division*

and other purposes. Besides, gasoline autos were cheaper to buy and cheaper to maintain.

The machine invented by Karl Benz had won out by 1905, although steam and electric autos were produced for a few more years.

As more and more people drove autos, the auto began to change society. One of the first changes was the decline in the use of the horse and of the industries based on the horse. Many industries, big and small, depended on the horse. They included black-smith shops, stables that rented horses and car-

Auto manufacturing was one of the new industries that sprang up to replace those based on the horse. The Olds Motor Works was the first auto manufacturer in the U.S. *Oldsmobile Division*

riages, carriage makers, and firms that operated public coaches between cities.

Some of these industries started making autos themselves. Studebaker Brothers Manufacturing Company in Indiana, a carriage maker, became a leading automobile maker.

As old industries based on the horse died, new ones based on the auto sprang up. One was the auto manufacturing industry itself. At the turn of the century there were thirty auto makers in the United States alone! Firms that made bodies and parts used by autos grew along with the auto industry. Small businesses, such as service stations that served the driver directly, soon arrived.

By 1908, the brand-new automobile industry and the firms connected with it were putting more

money into the U.S. economy than the horse industry. That same year, one of the new United States auto manufacturing firms introduced what was to become the most famous auto ever known. The Model T Ford would make the United States the number one auto-owning country in the world.

After that, nothing was quite the same.

3

Henry Ford and the American Auto

EARLY ON THE morning of June 4, 1896, Henry Ford completed his first automobile. Ford and his friend, Jim Bishop, looked proudly at the little car, which was in a brick shed behind Ford's rented house in Detroit, Michigan. It had four bicycle wheels, a single bicycle seat, two speeds, no reverse, and no brake. The whole machine weighed only about 500 pounds.

To Ford and Bishop, who had been working for months on the auto every night after their regular workday ended, it was beautiful.

The two decided to make their first road test that very night. The sun had not yet come up, making it a perfect time to test a machine that

Henry Ford's first automobile. *Ford Motor Company*

would frighten horses, and probably a few people as well. In 1896, most people in the United States hadn't seen an automobile. Ford began to spin the flywheel, just as Karl Benz had started his gasoline-powered tricycle.

Suddenly Ford stopped. He had just realized that the auto, which had been built inside the shed, was too wide for the door. Ford hesitated, then grabbed an axe and knocked down part of the brick wall. He spun the flywheel again. When the motor was rumbling, he leaped in the seat and pushed the lever used to steer. The little machine moved out of the shed and down the street.

Ford took only a short ride that June night, but it was enough to convince him that his machine was a success. The brick wall? Before Ford had a chance to rebuild it, his landlord saw the damage. He was so fascinated by the auto that he allowed his tenant to permanently enlarge the door. You can still see the brick shed with the enlarged door at Greenfield Village in Dearborn, Michigan.

Henry Ford was an engineer with Detroit Edison, the electric utility in the Detroit area, when he developed his first car. In 1899, with the backing of some wealthy men in the area, he formed the Detroit Automobile Company. Then he faced a hard choice. His superiors at Detroit Edison wanted to make him superintendent of the whole company. It was a good job, but it would leave him no time for the Detroit Automobile Company.

"I chose the automobile," he said later. He resigned from Detroit Edison.

The Model T was the car almost anyone could afford. *Ford Motor Company*

Ford was involved with two automobile manufacturing firms before he formed the Ford Motor Company in 1903. The third company produced an auto Ford called the Model A. It cost $750—$850 with a back seat. By the end of 1903, the Ford Motor Company was already making big profits.

The Model A and models that followed it were not expensive. But Ford wanted to make a good auto almost anyone could afford. "We'll build more of them and cheaper; better and cheaper," he said to one of his associates. And they did. His Model N cost only $500. Ford began to sell more autos than anyone else in the world.

In 1908, Henry Ford introduced the most famous car the world has ever known: the Model T Ford. Sales soared. Soon this one auto, or car, accounted for half the car sales in the United States! It was the only car Ford made from 1908 until 1927, and he eventually turned out fifteen million of them.

What made the Model T such a popular car? It was cheap, of course—and it got even cheaper. But the Model T had other advantages. It was light, it was sturdy, it was reliable, and it was easy to repair. Ford made sure that parts for the car were widely available. You could buy parts for Lizzie, as it was called, in the dime store or order them from Sears, Roebuck.

The first Lizzies were not as cheap as Henry Ford had hoped. They cost about $850. But he soon thought of a way to make them cheaper. At that time, each car was put together by a few skilled craftsmen. The parts to make the car were often bought from other firms. Ford began buying firms to make his own parts. Then he made sure that the parts were exactly like each other.

Now Ford was ready for the final step: the assembly line. He didn't invent this concept, but he used it better than anyone had before. In his new plant in Highland Park, Illinois, parts were brought to workmen by an overhead conveyor that moved just as fast as the men could work. Each workmen did only one part of the job.

If the magneto that started the engine required twenty-nine different steps to assemble, for instance, Ford assigned twenty-nine men to do the job. Each did one small part.

The assembly line made it possible to produce cars better and cheaper. *Ford Motor Company*

By 1914, it took only an hour and one half of one man's time to assemble the body of a Model T, compared to twelve and one half hours before. There were savings in time and manpower in other assembly jobs, too. Model Ts cost $850 in 1908, $600 in 1913, and $440 in 1915. Each auto cost Henry Ford more to make, because of the cost of the new machinery for the assembly line, but he sold so many cars he made more money.

Henry Ford's auto had such a huge effect on American society that it sometimes seems as though Ford invented the auto. But he wasn't even the first American to build a gasoline-powered car. In 1893, two brothers from Springfield, Massachusetts,

The first Oldsmobile dates from 1897. *Oldsmobile Division*

General Motors produced a range of models, one at each price.
This is their 1926 Pontiac. *General Motors*

Frank and Charles Duryea, built and ran a gasoline car. Frank drove a Duryea car to victory in the first auto race in the United States in 1895.

Henry Ford wasn't even the first American to build an inexpensive gasoline car. In 1900, Ransom Olds built a small one-cylinder car, the Oldsmobile, that sold for just $650.

The year the Ford Motor Company was founded, 1903, there were hundreds of other auto makers in the United States. Only a few prospered. One was Henry Ford's. Another was General Motors. GM, which was founded in 1908, got its start by buying the Buick Company. Later it bought Cadillac and Olds.

In the 1920s GM used Ford's production techniques to produce a range of models, at different prices. The models were changed every year. A former GM vice-president, Walter Chrysler, used the same policies at Chrysler. GM became the most profitable carmaker in the United States in 1924, a position it held for many years.

The model T was retired in 1927. Before long, Ford was offering a range of cars with models that changed every year, just like GM.

By 1915, there were over two million autos in the United States. Suddenly Americans became aware of a big problem: bad roads. Most of our roads were dirt. Cars bogged down in mud in rainy weather and were surrounded by clouds of dust in dry weather. "The American who buys an automobile finds himself with this great difficulty," wrote

Roads were bad in the United States in the early days of the car. *Michigan Department of Transportation*

Albert A. Pope, an early carmaker. "He has nowhere to use it."

In 1921, The Federal Highway Act was passed by the U.S. Congress. It gave money to the states to build paved roads. States and counties began passing bond issues to build their own roads. Special taxes and tolls paid for the roads. A network of good roads began to cover the United States.

4

Beautiful, Fast, and Expensive

EMIL JELLINEK, THE Austro-Hungarian consul at Nice, France, and a Daimler dealer, knew what he wanted in a car. Something long, low, and fast, he wrote to the Daimler Company in 1900. The car should go "forty kilometers per hour"—about 25 miles per hour. The Daimler Company objected, even though Jellinek was on their board of directors. Only racing cars went that fast. It wouldn't be safe.

But Jellinek was firm. The German company gave him what he wanted. The new car was full of innovations, all of which have become standard on today's cars. They included a steel body, a mechanism that made it easier to change gears, and a honeycomb radiator, so called because it looked something like a honeycomb. The tiny metal tubes

Twelve-year-old Mercedes Jellinek, for whom the Mercedes-Benz was named. *Daimler-Benz*

The 1901 Mercedes-Benz was long, low, and white. *Daimler-Benz*

that made up the comb did a better job of cooling the engine.

The new car was long, low, and white. And it was very fast indeed for those days. In a road race held in 1901, the new car averaged 35 miles per hour.

Jellinek, pleased, named the car for his twelve-year-old daughter, Mercedes. He quickly sold thirty-six of the new cars to his wealthy friends. Soon everyone was talking about the Mercedes. The name Mercedes became so well known that the car was still called Mercedes Benz after Daimler merged with the firm of Karl Benz in 1926 to become Daimler-Benz.

The Mercedes was the first of a special type of car—the luxury car. The people who bought the Mercedes didn't buy it simply to get from place to place. They bought it because it was beautiful and powerful and used the latest technology. Cost didn't matter. In 1901, the Mercedes sold for over $4,000— a high price for a car then. Today they range in price from $24,000 to $59,000.

The most famous luxury car of all first appeared in Britain in 1906. Henry Royce, the car's designer, was an electrical engineer like Henry Ford. He bought a French car for his own use, but it proved to be a "lemon"—a car with mechanical problems. Instead of fixing it, Royce created his own car.

A young British aristocrat, Charles Rolls, became Royce's partner, and the two introduced the first Rolls-Royce at an auto show. The silver-painted car ran so silently it was called the "Silver Ghost."

This Silver Ghost from 1907 still runs. *Rolls-Royce Motors*

Charles Rolls wins the 1906 Tourist Trophy race in Britain with the first Rolls-Royce. *Rolls-Royce Motors*

The Silver Ghost didn't have the innovations of the Mercedes, the Panhard, or the Model T. "I invent nothing," Royce once said. Instead, he put into his car the best features of other cars.

The Silver Ghost was such a success in the luxury-car market that this one model continued in production for nineteen years—as long as the Model T.

The Rolls-Royce is the most expensive car you can buy. The cheapest one costs over $100,000, and the most expensive model costs almost $200,000. One reason why these cars cost so much is that many skilled craftsmen are used to make them. This is true even today. Rolls-Royce boasts that only ten men in the world can make its radiator grille. They do all the work by hand.

A car like a Ford or a Chevrolet, on the other hand, is produced with the mass production techniques pioneered by Henry Ford. Most of the workers are not craftsmen, and machines do much of the work. But the cars produced by Rolls seem to have impressed Henry Ford. After he became wealthy, he bought a Rolls-Royce for himself.

The best-known luxury car made in the United States, the Cadillac, is even older than the Rolls. The firm that became Cadillac was founded by Henry Ford. After Ford left this firm, the second one with which he was connected, it was taken over by another Henry, Henry Leland. He changed the name to Cadillac Motor Car Company for Antoine Cadillac, who founded Detroit in 1701. The firm was bought by General Motors in 1908.

The 1930s Cadillacs were among the most elegant cars ever made. *General Motors*

Cadillac made several breakthroughs in auto technology. The most important was the self-starter. Luxury cars, like low-priced cars, had to be started with a crank, although it was often a chauffeur who did the cranking. Henry Leland put his engineers to work on the problem, and they soon had a starter which operated on the flywheel. Inventor Charles Kettering developed a special motor to run the self-starter.

Cadillac introduced the self-starter in 1912, and soon every car was using it. The industry had an agreement that a patent taken out by one maker could be used by all the others, so any innovation spread quickly.

Self-starters put more women behind the wheel. It required arm strength to crank an internal combustion engine, so many women left the driving to men. With the self-starter, more women were able to drive. Before long, women's full, floor-length dresses had been replaced by shorter, slimmer clothing in which it was easier to drive. The car helped change women's dress.

Luxury cars are just one kind of special car. Another kind is the racing car. The first real auto race was held in 1895 in France. It was won by Emil Levassor in a Panhard. His top speed was about eighteen miles per hour. The same year, Frank Duryea drove a Duryea to victory in the first auto race in the United States. There was snow on the ground, and Duryea averaged only five miles per hour!

The first races were run over roads used by other traffic. After a number of spectators were killed in a race in 1903, races were restricted to a course that was closed to other traffic or to a special track. The most famous road race is the Grand Prix, run over a long, winding course in France. The most famous track race is the Indianapolis 500, run around the Motor Speedway in Indianapolis, Indiana.

In the beginning, racing cars weren't really special. They were ordinary cars made for the average driver. But soon designers were modifying cars to make them go faster in races. Today racers are small, streamlined cars with special features such as "wings." These wings, or airfoils, push the car down so it holds the road better.

Some racing cars are designed for certain types

Bobby Rahal, winner of the 1986 Indianapolis 500. Note "wings" on front of car. *Indianapolis Motor Speedway*

of racing. Drag racers compete against one other car on a short, straight track. These racers are long and skinny. Speed racers don't compete against any other car; they race with the clock to see how fast they can go. In 1979, a speed racer with a rocket-powered engine reached 739 miles an hour. Rocket-powered speed racers look like planes without wings.

Many features first used on racers are now used on the cars we drive. In 1914, a Peugeot competing in a Grand Prix race was the first to use four-wheel brakes. Until then, cars had used brakes only on the rear wheels. The four-wheel brakes worked very well, and later this same car won the Indianapolis 500. Soon all racers and then all cars were equipped with four-wheel brakes.

5

How The Car
Changed The
World Around Us

BY 1930, CARS were more comfortable and easier
to drive. They had closed bodies, balloon tires, and
four-wheel brakes. The 1928 Cadillac introduced a
type of transmission that made gear shifting much
simpler. Twenty-nine million cars were registered in
the United States in 1930! That was seventy-seven
percent of all the cars registered in the world.

Our automobile industry produced eighty-five
percent of the world's cars.

Cars changed life all over the world, and
changed it very fast. But nowhere were the changes
bigger than in the United States, because we had
the most cars. The car changed where people

By 1930, there were twenty-nine million cars registered in the United States. *U.S. Department of Transportation*

worked, lived, and shopped. It changed what they did in their leisure time. It changed where children went to school. The car even changed how our country looked.

There were so many changes and they came so fast that it was like a revolution—a car revolution.

One of the biggest changes was in the places people lived. As soon as cars were readily available, many city residents who could afford to buy houses moved to the suburbs. The car made it possible for them to drive to their work in the city. There were suburbs before the automobile, but these early suburbs grew up near railroad stations or streetcar stops. The new suburbs were everywhere.

As city residents moved to the suburbs, shops and other small businesses followed them. A new

Cars surround the Southdale Center in Edina, Minnesota, the first enclosed shopping center in the country. *Equitable's Prime Property Fund*

kind of shopping area, the shopping center, first appeared in a suburb of Kansas City, Missouri, in the 1920s. Customers, most of whom arrived by car, parked in special areas. Shops in many cities lost customers to the shopping centers.

Repair garages and service stations appeared in suburban areas to keep the suburbanites' cars running.

The car changed rural life, too. Before the car, farm families had to drive a horse and carriage a long way to a post office to pick up their mail. The car made delivery to every rural mailbox possible. Farm families also used their cars—or a small truck—for shopping and visiting. These families were not isolated the way they had been before the era of the car.

Service stations followed city dwellers to the suburbs. *Exxon Company*

The car made delivery to every rural mailbox possible. *National Archives*

The car changed rural life in another way. At the end of my street is a one-room schoolhouse. It closed in 1928, when children began going to a big "consolidated school" by bus. The same change from one-room schoolhouses to consolidated schools took place all over the United States as buses became available.

As soon as the car was widely available, it seemed as though everyone in the United States was taking vacations by car. There were no motels at first, so tourists camped out or rented rooms from farmers. The first tourist cabins, which opened after World War I, were tiny buildings with just room enough for a bed. But they cost only one dollar a night!

Soon chains of restaurants and motels sprang up to serve the new tourists. Howard Johnson opened its first roadside restaurants in Massachusetts in the 1930s. TraveLodge opened the first of the chain motels in California during World War II. Some drivers didn't need motels or restaurants. They attached homemade trailers to their cars. The manufacture of trailers and motor homes became a business.

One of the first places the early tourists headed for was our national parks. Most national parks are in remote spots, so they had few visitors before the car. The car made our national parks the popular vacation spots they are today. In 1904, the first year statistics were kept, only 120,690 people visited national parks. In 1930, the parks had over 3,000,000 visitors.

In 1938, when this car visited Hot Springs National Park, the national parks had over six million visitors. *National Park Service*

Some people didn't need motels. *National Park Service*

To serve all these drivers, the states, with the help of the federal government, built more and more highways. The biggest public works project ever created in the United States was the result of the 1956 Highway Aid Act. It authorized a system of interstate highways that would cover forty-one thousand miles and link every major city in the United States. A tax on gasoline and oil paid for the highways. The system will be completed in the 1990s.

Many of these changes made our world a better place to live and work and play. But some of the changes have been bad ones. Billboards and the commercial "strips" that have grown up along highways make parts of our cities and rural areas ugly. Badly planned highways split towns, destroy neighborhoods, and replace historic buildings.

As more highways are built, more cars use them. Traffic congestion in countries with many cars grows worse every year. One traffic expert figured that a car in a big-city rush hour moves more slowly than a horse and carriage! And now that corporations and other businesses have moved to the suburbs, traffic jams are no longer confined to cities.

Traffic creates other problems, too. The major source of outdoor noise in cities and towns comes from traffic. Car exhausts in traffic give off pollutants that can affect people's health. In areas like Los Angeles, hydrocarbons, one type of pollutant found in car exhausts, cause smog. Smog harms plants as well as people.

The use of mass transit decreased due to cars.

Strips make some highways ugly. *Barbara Ford*

When cars became available, train ridership dropped. At the same time, federal and state governments reduced their spending on trains and tracks. Trains deteriorated, losing more passengers. Many of our trains have gone out of service. Service on most streetcar lines was ended because their tracks interfered with car traffic.

The car contributed to the social problems of our cities. After city residents who could afford to buy houses moved to the suburbs, poor people were left behind. Many of them lost their jobs when businesses that employed them left the city too. Central cities became populated by large numbers of poor people, many of them unemployed. When highways were built through cities, some poor people lost their homes.

Cars also made the United States dependent on foreign oil. We used to produce most of the oil we use, but in the 1960s our oil imports from the Middle East began to climb. More than half our oil is refined into gasoline. We need lots of gasoline because we not only have more cars, but, before 1980, most of our cars were big, with powerful engines. Such cars need more gas.

The worst problem caused by the car is the number of deaths and injuries that result from car accidents. By the 1930s, more than thirty thousand people in the United States were being killed in car accidents each year. States improved roads, put up better traffic signs, and passed strict traffic laws. The rate of deaths dropped. But each year, the total number of deaths climbed as more Americans drove cars.

6

Living With The Car

IN THE MID-1950s, a hitchhiker on a Massachusetts highway saw an accident in which a baby had
been killed. When the car in which it had been
riding struck another car, the baby was hurled for-
ward. The door of the glove compartment flew open
and sliced through the baby's neck like a knife.

The hitchhiker was Harvard University law
student Ralph Nader. He never forgot the scene on
the Massachusetts highway. In 1965, Nader, now a
lawyer, testified before a U.S. Senate committee
headed by Senator Abraham Ribicoff. The young
lawyer described flaws in the design of U.S. cars that
made them unsafe to drive. Nader's book on car
safety, *Unsafe at Any Speed*, was published the same
year.

The testimony before the committee and Na-

President Lyndon B. Johnson signs National Traffic and Motor Vehicle Safety Act in 1966. *National Archives*

der's book led to the first federal law regulating the way cars are designed. In 1966, President Lyndon B. Johnson signed the Traffic and Motor Vehicle Safety Act into law. The law gave a new federal agency, the National Highway Traffic Safety Administration, the responsibility for reducing car accidents.

The NHTSA sets safety standards for all cars sold in this country. The standards make it mandatory for cars to have features like seat belts, locks that prevent doors from flying open in a crash, and sturdy bumpers that protect the car's frame. The NHTSA also participates in other safety activities, such as driver education.

Many people are still killed on U.S. highways. But if we look at the number of deaths for every one hundred million miles traveled, less than half as many people are killed each year as were in 1966.

Crash! It looks like an accident but it's really a safety test conducted by Calspon Corporation for the NHTSA. Tests like these help the NHTSA develop safety standards for cars.
Calspon Corporation

General Motors uses dummies like these in its safety research.
General Motors

Legislation has helped reduce the effects of some other car problems, too. In 1970, Congress passed the Clean Air Act. Under this act, all cars sold in the United States after 1975 must be equipped with a device called the catalytic converter. The converter reduces carbon monoxide and hydrocarbons in car exhaust. Cars with converters can't use gas with lead, so no-lead gas is now sold at service stations.

The most far-reaching law affecting cars, the Energy Policy and Conservation Act, was passed in 1975. It requires yearly changes in the fuel efficiency of cars—the miles a car can drive on a gallon of gas. The goal of the law was a fuel efficiency of 27.5 miles per gallon by 1985. Not every car had to achieve that mileage; the figure is the average for all models sold by a car manufacturer.

This was a big change for American cars. The average American car of that period weighed two tons and got 15 miles to the gallon. European cars averaged 25 miles to the gallon. European cars were much smaller than American cars, had less powerful engines, and used manual transmission in which gears were shifted by hand. To reach an average of 27.5 miles per gallon, U.S. car manufacturers would have to make some of their cars the same way.

The 1975 law was passed because of OPEC, the Organization of Petroleum Exporting Countries. Many of these countries are in the Middle East, which has large oil reserves. In 1973, OPEC raised the price of oil sharply. Suddenly gas wasn't cheap anymore. In the United States, we realized for the first time how dependent we were on oil from the Middle East. The oil price rise not only affected our cars, but our electric power system, which depends partly on oil, and the homes that use oil for heat.

In 1978, there was another round of price increases from OPEC, which also lowered production. This time the effects were much worse. Supplies of gasoline ran low at many service stations across the United States. Long lines of cars waited in line to buy gasoline. New Jersey, my state, issued a regulation: drivers with license plates ending in even numbers could buy gas only on even-numbered days, drivers with plates ending in odd numbers only on odd-numbered days.

My husband commuted seventy miles to work and back from our home in a distant suburb. "We need a car with better mileage," he said. The cars with the best mileage for the price, we found, were small foreign makes with Oriental names like Toyota, Nissan, and Honda. For the past ten years, Japan had been gearing up its small passenger-car industry. Now it was ready to sell Americans the kind of car we didn't make ourselves—small, reliable, with good mileage.

We bought a Toyota with a four-cylinder engine and a manual transmission in 1978. The four-cylinder engine sounded strange compared to our six-cylinder American car, but it got thirty-three miles to the gallon.

By 1980, Toyota was the leading car manufacturer in the world, surpassing the United States. Toyota is still number one. Sales of small European

The fuel-efficient Volkswagen "Beetle," made in Germany, is the kind of car we didn't make ourselves—until recently.
Volkswagon

cars, some of which had been available in the United States for a number of years, soared during this period too. Sales of big American cars dropped. GM, Ford, and Chrysler, burdened with stocks of big cars, lost huge sums of money. Chrysler almost went bankrupt.

American carmakers, who had been designing cars to meet the provisions of the 1975 law, quickly introduced their own versions of the fuel-efficient car. Most of them were made in Japan. Chrysler's "subcompacts," as small cars are called here, did so well that the firm, under the leadership of Lee Iacocca, became a success again. All three of our big car manufacturers are making money today.

The 1986 Chevrolet Sprint gets sixty miles to the gallon on the highway. *General Motors*

In 1986, GM introduced its Sprint models, which get sixty miles to the gallon on the highway. That's the best mileage for any car sold in the United States.

American carmakers still make big cars, and so do firms like Daimler-Benz and Rolls-Royce. As long as there are people who can afford big luxury cars, carmakers will continue to turn them out. But even big cars like the Cadillac are smaller than they used to be. Today manufacturers like GM and Daimler-Benz conduct their own research on fuel efficiency, safety, and pollution-control devices.

In the future, carmakers tell us, cars will be lighter and more streamlined, making them still more fuel efficient. They'll be safer too, as the result of computer devices that will control cars in a skid and alert the driver to dangers on the road ahead.

The car of the 1990's may look like this research car designed by the Pontiac Division of General Motors. *Pontiac Division*

Chevrolet's streamlined experimental car "Express" is designed for use on special highways. *Chevrolet Division*

We may even turn to another type of engine—possibly an electric engine that would be pollution-free. One electric car available today can run for sixty miles without being recharged. It has a top speed of fifty-five miles per hour.

We're finding ways to deal with some other car problems, too. In 1986, plans to build a new highway through the busiest area of New York City were shelved when opponents of the plan won a lawsuit. More attention is being paid to community concerns and the environment. States and cities are putting money into mass transit to relieve the congestion on highways. Congress is considering a new law to control billboards.

We have to find solutions to the problems created by cars, because the horseless carriage will always be with us in some form. We can no longer get along without it.

Index

Seat belts, 47
Self-starter, 34, 35
Service stations, 2, 14, 18, 39
"Silver Ghost," 31–33. *See also* Rolls-Royce
Steering wheels, 12
Studebaker Brothers Manufacturing Co., 18
Système Panhard, 9

Tiller, 2
Tires, 13, 14–15, 37
Toyota, 50

Traffic, 35, 43, 45
Trailers, 41–42
Trains, 2, 6, 16, 38, 44. *See also* Mass transit
Transmission, 37
TraveLodge, 41

Unsafe at Any Speed (Nader), 46–47

Wheels, 1, 3, 13, 14
Windshields, 10
"Wings," 35